ASTICOU AZALEA GARDEN

THE WORK OF CHARLES K. SAVAGE

BY

LETITIA S. BALDWIN

MOUNT DESERT LAND & GARDEN PRESERVE

ASTICOU AZALEA GARDEN AND THUYA GARDEN
are owned and operated by the Mount Desert Land & Garden Preserve
and are part of a larger 140-acre land parcel that includes the Asticou
Terraces and a public landing on the eastern shore of Northeast Harbor.
Formerly called The Island Foundation, the nonprofit organization was
founded in 1971 by David and Peggy Rockefeller as a future repository
for some of their Maine land holdings. The Asticou Azalea Garden has
been a part of the Garden Preserve since 1973; the Thuya properties
joined the Garden Preserve in 2000. Both gardens conform to sustain-
able organic gardening practices. The privately-owned Abby Aldrich
Rockefeller Garden and many acres of land that lie between Seal Harbor
and Thuya Garden will eventually become part of the preserve.

ISBN 978-0-9818104-0-9

Contents

Rhododendron japonicum

Foreword

I was born in San Francisco, and Japan always seemed very close. The prints of the "mustard-seed garden" were on my bedroom walls and Japanese blue and white bowls always held the luscious persimmons of fall. So when I first discovered the carefully raked path to the Azalea Garden, I felt suddenly at home. Dr. Thomas Hall and Patrick Chassé had just restored Charles Savage's beautiful garden, and Tom would spend most days there, talking with visitors and explaining the philosophy of Japanese gardening. We became friends, and together hired Mary Roper, our head gardener.

That was nineteen years ago. Since then Mary has visited Kyoto and studied there, we have had Yuji Yoshimura and Ivan Watters prune the garden in true Japanese style, and always, a devoted garden committee reinforcing the support of the Island Foundation, now the Mount Desert Land & Garden Preserve.

The year 2008 is the fiftieth anniversary of both the Thuya and the Azalea gardens created by Charles Savage, and we want to pay tribute to his genius. These books by Letitia Baldwin will give you the history of both gardens. I hope you will enjoy them.

Beth Straus
Honorary Chair
Asticou Azalea Garden Committee

Island Garden

SEEN FROM AFAR, the Mount Desert hills rise from the sea. As the sun spreads its early morning light, soaring cliffs turn rose, gold, umber and violet. Ray by luminous ray, the blue dawn picks out fjord, mountain, pond and glistening lake nestled among its glacially carved valleys.

Whether on the jagged summit of Cadillac Mountain, coastal Maine's highest peak, or deep within the island's forests, an array of lime-green, cadmium-orange and slate-blue lichens creates an extraordinary tapestry of color on the pink granite outcrops. Battered by wind and salt spray, bonsai-like pitch pine cling to the rocky crevices.

Rhodora, juniper, sheep laurel and other native shrubs border more than one hundred miles of the island's hiking trails and walking paths, most within the boundaries of Acadia National Park. Lush ferns and velvety mosses line brooks and streams. White-flowered bunchberry carpets fragrant fir-spruce forests with glossy leaves and scarlet berries. Water lilies and pickerelweed, like Japanese floral designs, skirt the edges of ponds.

Mount Desert Island is itself like a Japanese garden. It's no wonder that few formal gardens come close to matching the island's wild, perennial beauty. The Asticou Azalea Garden, with its rare blossoms and unusual contours creating quiet, intimate vistas at the head of Northeast Harbor, surely does, drawing thousands of people each year from around the globe.

Starting in mid-May, visitors to the Azalea Garden stroll amid clouds of blossoming crabapple trees and past rounded banks of rhododendrons, whose pastel hues are reflected in a central pond. In the moss garden, the cushiony, iridescent green mounds tempt touch. Farther along, ancient granite rocks rise like islands from a sea of rippled white sand. Upturned clay roof tiles form a wave pattern between weathered stone slabs. Around the bend, a small clutch of sand myrtle, marsh marigold and dwarf ferns catches the eye.

Charles Kenneth Savage (1903-1979), whose grandfather founded Northeast Harbor's Asticou Inn in 1883, designed both the Asticou Azalea Garden and neighboring Thuya Garden in the mid-1950s. These two major life works, located within a quarter-mile of each other on Peabody Drive in Northeast Harbor, share the distinction of having been created from plantings salvaged from legendary American landscape designer Beatrix Farrand's dismantled Bar Harbor estate, Reef Point.

Savage, who had abandoned plans to study architecture and landscape design due to his father's premature death, devoted himself instead to running his family's inn from 1922 to 1964. But the

artistically gifted man never gave up his own interests. He traveled the world through books, educating himself about far-ranging topics from botany to the fine art of lettering, tapping the minds of mentors like Farrand, Boston landscape architect Joseph H. Curtis, John D. Rockefeller, Jr., sculptor R. Tait McKenzie and other notable people who either stayed at the inn or summered on Mount Desert Island.

This self-taught garden designer genuinely saw Mount Desert Island as a garden and delighted in its natural compositions, from a mountaintop partially eclipsed by fog to pine cones randomly scattered on the forest floor. He wanted others to enjoy and treasure the unique Maine landscape as he did, but to tread lightly and treat it reverently.

A FUSION OF EAST AND WEST

The Asticou Azalea Garden is Savage's distillation of the woods and craggy mountaintops of his beloved Maine isle. Savage was also inspired by the water garden at Katsura Imperial Villa in Kyoto. As in that famed Japanese garden, visitors to the Azalea Garden stroll along a circular path through a series of verdant rooms. A granite-slab bridge, strikingly accented by upright stones, spans a meandering stream. Mown lawns rise above a small reflecting pond.

Deepening this connection between East and West is the presence of Beatrix Farrand's unusual plant collection, said to be the finest north of the Arnold Arboretum. Her influence is visible in the carefully composed succession of colors and textures throughout the seasons and in the seamless weaving of hardy exotics such as rare alpine azaleas with pitch pine, hair cap moss and other indigenous plantings. Farrand's greatest contribution to this garden, though, are her botanical treasures painstakingly raised from seed sent to Reef Point from places as distant as Sweden and Kashmir.

LEFT: *Asticou Inn, one of the Savage family businesses and hub of summer season social and intellectual activities in Northeast Harbor since the late 1800s, circa 1920s.*

BELOW: *Charles K. Savage on a family vacation in Florida, circa 1919.*

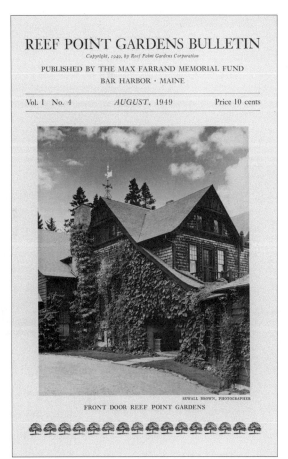

REEF POINT GARDENS BULLETIN

Copyright, 1949, by Reef Point Gardens Corporation

PUBLISHED BY THE MAX FARRAND MEMORIAL FUND
BAR HARBOR · MAINE

Vol. I No. 4   *AUGUST*, 1949   Price 10 cents

SEWALL BROWN, PHOTOGRAPHER

FRONT DOOR REEF POINT GARDENS

Paula Deitz, who edits *The Hudson Review* and writes about gardens for the *New York Times* and other publications, knows both the garden and Farrand's legacy well, having summered in the nearby town of Blue Hill for years. She wrote the introduction to a compilation of Farrand's work, *Beatrix Farrand: The Bulletins of Reef Point Gardens*.[1] Deitz believes that Savage's fusion of Eastern and Western garden design is unique.

"One can only imagine the remarkable convergence of events that initiated Charles Savage's creative decision to transform the dormant water meadow across from the Asticou Inn into a flourishing Japanese-style garden, thus preserving Beatrix Farrand's valuable plants, primarily the azaleas, in a new and artful setting. Beyond the understandable pressure among Mrs. Farrand's friends to find a new home for her collection, there was Mr. Savage's own recognition that the natural coastal scenery of Mount Desert Island had similarities with the aesthetics of the Japanese stroll garden: strewn boulders, blankets of moss and brilliant autumnal color. He read about these gardens and took elements from Katsura and the sand garden at Ryoan-ji to design a version he

on the Thompson Island Bridge. "This Bridge is dedicated to the Soldiers, Sailors and Marines of Hancock County," reads the commemorative tablet tucked in the northwest corner of the span crossing over Mount Desert Narrows.

The World War I memorial, a tribute to the region's soldiers, is finely lettered and shows an American eagle with wings spread and bordered by white pine boughs, cones and pine needles. In 1918, at the age of fifteen, Charles designed the bas-relief and won fifty dollars in gold coins thanks to an islandwide public school contest. Inspired by the nineteenth-century American sculptor Augustus Saint-Gaudens, the gifted Maine teen made pencil sketches and executed his design in sepia ink on Bristol board. "It reflects the fervor of the time and the symbol of the state of Maine," Charles Savage later wrote.[2]

As part of his winnings, Savage was credited as the designer on the memorial. He, however, had

Eastern dry garden landscapes are often reminiscent of oceanscapes such as this view from Cadillac Mountain.

OPPOSITE: *Savage family, circa 1900, including Emily Manchester Savage (seated in porch rocker, left) and A.C. Savage (seated in porch chair, right)—paternal grandparents of Charles K. Savage.*

would call 'parallel rather than imitative' of the Kyoto gardens. With proper pruning and maintenance by equally inspired gardeners and overseers—and enriched by the patina of time—the Asticou Azalea Garden has been recognized among the great treasures of New England gardens."

SEAFARING ROOTS

Most motorists crossing over to Mount Desert Island from the mainland would be hard-pressed to notice a small bronze plaque that is mounted his name filed off the plaque later in life. No one who knew him well is surprised by this. Savage's life was characterized by quiet service to others.

Born on February 2, 1903, at his maternal grandparents' home in the Washington County town of Milbridge, some thirty miles downeast of Northeast Harbor, Savage was the eldest son of George A. and Mabelle S. Savage. Both parents were descended from British seafarers. His mother's forebears were sea captains and master shipbuilders in the Milbridge area. The Savage family descended from Sarah and John Savage, a Revolutionary War veteran who cleared shorefront and built a log cabin at Harbor Brook in 1798, becoming one of the town of Mount Desert's early white settlers.

At the head of Northeast Harbor, in the hairpin turn where the Asticou Inn stands today, a coral-colored clapboard house hugs the inland roadside. Harbor Cottage, now a hotel guesthouse called Cranberry Lodge, was the heart of Savage family life throughout the latter part of the nineteenth and early twentieth centuries. From his wooden rocker on the front porch, Capt. Augustus Chase Savage (1832-1911), known to family members as A.C., could see over the rye field and down to his family's wharf, where the coastal schooners he either owned or had a share in, loaded spruce wood and other cargo bound for Boston, New York and points elsewhere.

"The place consisted of a few farming and fishing households, whose principal contact with one another would have been by rowboat or by walking along the shore," Savage wrote in a posthumous foreword to his grandfather's 1902 memoir, *Memories of a Lifetime.* "It is difficult indeed to comprehend the utter stillness which was here in 1832 and the immediate years following. A call or 'hello' from some man to attract a neighbor's attention, the moo of a cow, the sound of a sheep and the clucking of hens; the wind, the distant roar of the sea on a southeaster, an occasional creak of a spar or flapping of a sail when near enough."

A charcoal drawing of the Asticou Inn as viewed from the street, by Scott White, circa 1959.

RIGHT: *The Asticou Inn and its sloping grounds viewed from the shore, circa 1959.*

Charles Savage's life revolved around Asticou, a neighborhood wrapping around Northeast Harbor's upper reaches, where his enterprising grandfather had the foresight to open the Asticou Inn in the late nineteenth century. A.C. and his wife Emily had previously hosted seasonal visitors in their home. These visitors were captivated by the island's unmatched vistas of sea and mountains and also charmed by a rustic warmth epitomized by the Savage household.

Among the very first guests at Harbor Cottage were the highly regarded nineteenth-century landscape painters George Hollingsworth and Harrison B. Brown. They were soon followed by Boston landscape architect Joseph H. Curtis and Harvard President Charles W. Eliot, who came with their families. They delighted in Emily's delicious fish chowder, yeast rolls and gingerbread and must have been entertained, too, by A.C.'s dry wit and tales of towering icebergs in the Belle Isle Strait and being caught in a gale near Minot's Ledge off Cohasset, Massachusetts.

The pleasure, of course, was mutual. A.C. and Emily, who had six children, found the Eliots and Curtises wonderfully stimulating. A friendship blossomed between the Maine and Massachusetts families, all of whom treasured the elemental natural beauty of Maine. In 1880, the Bostonians purchased land from A.C. along Northeast Harbor's eastern shore. To build their shingle-style cottages, they asked none other than the innkeeper and his sons.

TRUE ARTISANS

As his cottage took shape, the Harvard president noticed that A.C.'s son Fred had a gift for cabinetry and woodcarving and arranged for the nineteen-year-old to apprentice at the Boston architectural firm of Peabody & Stearns. Fred began training in 1884 as a draftsman under architect Robert Swain Peabody and then started his own architectural practice at Asticou in 1886. Fred Savage became one of Maine's most prolific architects, best known for his shingle-style cottages that complemented the rugged coastal landscape.

LEFT: *The village of Asticou, with the Roberts House in the foreground and the original Asticou Inn behind, circa 1885.*

At the turn of the twentieth century, the sound of saw and hammer echoed through Northeast Harbor for months at a time. Wielding the tools were Fred, his father, A.C., and brothers Herman and George. Together they produced the dozens of cottages and several inns that gave the coastal village its character and made it one of the most exclusive summer resorts on the eastern seaboard.

When Fred Savage's nephews weren't digging for spruce gum, picking wild blueberries, hunting for arrowheads or exploring the hillside trails, Charles, his younger brother George and their cousins Emily and Augustus Phillips would head for the steamboat wharf. There, they delighted in watching the passengers disembark, especially those with mountains of steamer trunks packed for a stay of a month or more at the Asticou Inn or one of the other grand hotels in Northeast Harbor.

A.C. died in 1911, and George A. Savage (1873-1922), his third eldest surviving son, assumed ownership of the Asticou Inn. A portly man

with black curly hair and rosy cheeks, George relished his work. With Charles or George Jr. on his shoulder, he would sing "My Georgia Lady Love," his voice carrying over the hotel grounds.

Mabelle S. Savage (1877-1965), George's vivacious wife, was musical too, having studied piano at Crane's Music School in Boston. She taught Charles, George and her niece Emily to play the piano. A petite woman who dressed smartly in elegant hats and mink stoles, Mabelle was known for her custard pies and luscious chocolate cake. She took pains to arrange the lilies, snapdragons and other flowers from the Asticou Inn's cutting garden, passing on her love of flowers to her sons.

"She loved music. Loved jewelry, too. She played the piano so all her rings clanked up and down the keyboard," recalled Charles' daughter Mary Ann Savage Habib, who was appointed her grandmother's chauffeur in later years. "I think my father got his sense of humor from her and also his love of color and beautiful things."

Family of Charles Savage, circa 1921. Mother, Mabelle, and younger brother, George.

A CALL TO RETURN HOME

After graduating from Northeast Harbor's Gilman High School in 1921, Charles was sent to do post-secondary work at the elite, then all-boys Noble and Greenough School in Massachusetts. He intended to pursue an architectural degree at the Massachusetts Institute of Technology.

But Charles' plans were abruptly halted in March of 1922 by his father's sudden death at age forty-nine. As the eldest child, he was expected to fill his father's shoes and help his very capable, but demanding mother run the inn. Under circumstances that might have left another young man bitter, Charles returned to Maine and invested his fine aesthetic sensibility in the classic hotel, becoming involved in all phases of its operation, from menu design and property management to the artful placement of a bough of pitch pine in one of the Chinese bronze vessels he collected.

Devotion to family and to Mount Desert Island's natural beauty spurred his many artistic efforts and civic duties. He served as a selectman, state representative and local library trustee. He helped found the former Mount Desert Larger Par-

ish, comprising five churches, and presided over The Acadia Corporation, the private company that still operates the historic Jordan Pond House and several gift shops in Acadia National Park.

The innkeeper held formidable aesthetic standards for himself and others; for much of his life he served as the town's unofficial arbiter of design and taste. To him we owe the preservation of Jordan Pond House's charming tradition of tea and popovers and the striking absence of billboards and unsightly signage throughout town.

Savage wove design into every aspect of his daily life. He carved wooden signs and bas-reliefs of native flora and other island motifs by hand. He was a gifted watercolorist and landscape photographer. His refined hand is visible in such places as the Northeast Harbor Library, where his carved wooden panel depicting images from Chaucer's *The Canterbury Tales* still graces the mantelpiece.

Charles K. Savage watercolor of the Asticou Inn gardens, circa 1935.

RIGHT: *Hotel guest relaxing on the Asticou Inn porch, circa 1947.*

LEFT: *Guests of the Asticou Inn preparing for an afternoon carriage ride in Acadia National Park, circa 1926.*

That Savage managed to design and engineer the Thuya and Azalea gardens is remarkable, considering the breadth of his responsibilities in life. But the fact that he possessed the aesthetic sensibility and horticultural knowledge to create these living treasures is not so surprising, given the value his forebears placed on learning and their lively interest in and open-mindedness to the world beyond Maine. Northeast Harbor librarian, Robert R. Pyle, not only knew Charles Savage well, but also knew four generations of his family.

"All of the early families in Northeast Harbor have held in high value a practical education. The Savages of Asticou, however, added to practical learning a high appreciation for that which is artistic and aesthetic, and this pervades their contributions to their community. Whether it be in state and local government, in which at least one member of each generation has given time and energy; religious faith; education, which has also called at least one member of each generation from the late 1800s onward; or a range of musical or artistic expressions, the Savages—architects, landscape designer, musicians, educators, designers and executors of remarkable sculpted wood carvings—continue today to generate a wealth of betterment that enriches their community. It is a privilege to have known four generations of them."[3]

Savage was greatly helped and supported by his loving, highly capable wife, Katharine Larchar Savage (1905-2001). From Old Town, Maine, the University of Maine graduate met her husband while teaching home economics at the Gilman High School in Northeast Harbor. Katharine, like Charles, was a kind and painfully modest person who worked tirelessly behind the scenes at the inn, never seeking recognition. "It was up to Katharine to find her place in this Savage hometown and business," Marcia Savage, a niece and neighbor, wrote in Katharine's obituary.[4] "By the time her children were born, Katharine had found her place at the inn and built her own reputation for excel-

Katharine Savage strolling an island garden, circa 1999.

Rhododendron kaempferi

lence in its kitchen…Katharine arose at 4:00 a.m., donned a white uniform dress and baker's apron and headed for the hotel's basement bakery. Here she oversaw the kitchen staff and chefs and produced her own legendary dinner rolls, pies, creamy ice creams, sorbets and fruit desserts."

THE FARRAND LEGACY

As summer cottages proliferated, so did elaborate gardens on Mount Desert Island. Many that employed a more naturalistic approach were designed by Beatrix Farrand (1872-1959). During her renowned career, the American landscape designer carried out two hundred private and public commissions, including the White House East Garden, the New York Botanical Garden's Rose Garden and large areas of the Yale and Princeton campuses. Dumbarton Oaks, the Italianate gardens surrounding a nineteenth-century Federalist mansion in the Georgetown neighborhood of Washington, D.C., is her most famous work.

Farrand, whose parents hailed from old New York and Philadelphia families, grew up in New York City. She was an only child, the niece of nineteenth-century novelist Edith Wharton. When she was twelve, her parents divorced. Reef Point, her family's summer place in Bar Harbor since 1879, became Farrand's refuge and spiritual home. This six-acre property bordering Bar Harbor's Shore Path overlooked Frenchman Bay and the Porcupine

Islands. Cloaked in clematis, Chinese jasmine, wisteria, hydrangea and honeysuckle, the brown-shingled house blended with the landscape. The rose terraces, espaliered fruit trees, perennial borders, masses of azaleas, laurels and rhododendrons, and rock and bog gardens featuring native ferns, heath, sweet gale and Labrador tea were laid out in relation to ocean views framed by red and white spruce trees. Grass aisles, crossed by curvilinear paths, fanned out toward the sea.

Seemingly exotic apricot, salmon and scarlet azaleas thrived in the seaside setting. "They like the moisture from the sea and the old silver sand under their feet," Farrand wrote in her *Reef Point Gardens Bulletins,* a series of fifteen slim volumes published from 1946 to 1956 that detailed horticultural lessons learned at the center.

As Reef Point Gardens expanded, Farrand set about transforming her Bar Harbor property into an educational institution for aspiring landscape architects. Her botanical collection encompassed more than one thousand specimens from the far reaches of the world, and her vast library boasted over 2,700 horticultural and gardening books.

Besides commissions in New York, Connecticut and Washington, D.C., Farrand was much in demand as a landscape designer on Mt. Desert Island. In 1926, philanthropist John D. Rockefeller, Jr. and his wife Abby hired her to design a garden at The Eyrie, their half-timbered Tudor-style summer home atop Barr Hill in Seal Harbor.

Situated on a wooded granite bluff, the Abby Aldrich Rockefeller Garden is greatly influenced by the Rockefellers' lengthy journey to the Far East in 1921. A pink-washed stucco wall topped with yellow glazed tiles from China encloses a lavish flower garden. Ornamental borders frame a rectangular green. Curving garden walls are pierced by various portals, including the Bottle Gate and round Moon Gate. The Spirit Path, lined with striking Korean tomb figures and other stone sculptures, leads to a Buddhist votive stele from China. Hair cap moss, bunchberry, low-bush blueberry and other native ground covers spill over the path's edges and soften the effect.

An imposing, elegant woman often clad in Harris tweed suits and her signature black choker, Farrand became a familiar figure on Mount Desert during the four years it took to complete the Rockefeller garden. "In my youth, it was a common sight to see Mrs. Farrand being driven in her open car, with the top down, in season or out, on her visits of inspection," Savage later recalled. "Her work at Reef Point remains for me a precious recollection."[1]

During this same period, the famed landscape designer also could be seen riding with John D. Rockefeller, Jr. in his four-wheeled carriage on roadside tours through Acadia National Park. As his great carriage road system was being built, Rockefeller relied upon Farrand's advice about everything from plant restoration to the development of scenic views. The two would soon serve as mentors to a Northeast Harbor innkeeper who shared their passion for the island and was equally determined to preserve the island's rare natural beauty.

OPPOSITE PAGE:
Beatrix Farrand and "Cubby." California, 1934.

LEFT: Rhododendron catawbiense *'Roseum Elegans.'*

AN ERA CLOSES

In 1947, life changed irrevocably on Mount Desert Island. The summer and fall had been the driest on record, and forest fires had broken out all over Maine. The island had been spared until October 17, when, at 4:00 p.m., a Mrs. Gilbert spotted smoke rising from a cranberry bog in Bar

tates and one hundred seventy year-round homes. The town's property tax base was wiped out because many of the summer people simply never returned.

At the time of the fire, Bar Harbor's grand cottage era was already beginning to fade. The Great Depression altered the lifestyles of much of the summer colony, while America's growing love affair with the automobile made the Maine island much more accessible. By the 1950s, vacationers of more modest means were increasingly discovering Bar Harbor. The Asticou, like other grand inns, struggled to remain viable.

In Bar Harbor, Farrand's Reef Point Gardens survived the fire, but the designer was finding it nearly impossible to finance her horticultural study center and secure knowledgeable garden staff to preserve and perpetuate her work. She sought tax-exempt status from the town of Bar Harbor, but town officials, already grappling with reduced property tax revenue, denied her request.

Faced with an uncertain future, Farrand made the extraordinary decision to eliminate her creation rather than allow its demise over time. In 1955 she ordered her beloved childhood home torn down and sold the shorefront property. The University of California at Berkeley agreed to take her 2,700 books and hundreds of drawings. Savage, who served on the Reef Point Gardens Board of Directors, was among those who protested Farrand's

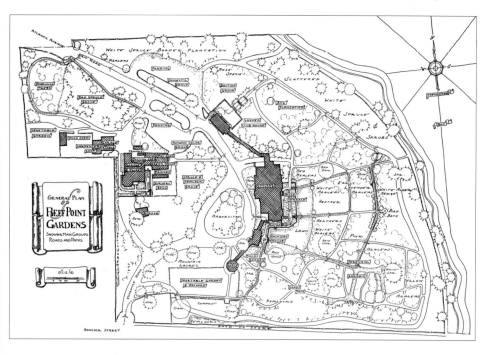

Map used for walking tours of the Reef Point Gardens, circa 1930.

Harbor. No one knows for sure how the fire began, but it continued smoldering underground, and days later, gale-force winds rekindled the flames and the blaze rebounded out of control. It took an entire month before the fire was declared out.

The Great Fire of '47 burned nearly half of the eastern side of the island, including five of Bar Harbor's historic hotels, sixty-seven summer es-

dramatic decision. "I was horrified and wrote at once in remonstrance, but to no avail," Savage said years later. [6]

Mount Desert Island architect Robert W. Patterson, Farrand's close friend and longtime colleague, bought Reef Point. The sale enabled Farrand to build a small cottage onto the farmhouse owned by her faithful staff, Lewis and Amy Magdalene Garland, in the Bar Harbor village of Salisbury Cove. She and her companion, Clementine Walter, lived there until Farrand's death in 1959.

LIVING ART

"It is commonplace to say that a garden is a living painting; it is not at all common to see one that has the quality of a good painting," Patterson wrote in 1959. "The Beatrix Farrand gardens did have that quality in their freedom and scale, their color and composition. But they were living things,

and those that survive will miss the painstaking hand and the unerring eye of the artist who created them."[7]

When Patterson offered Savage the option to buy Reef Point's plant material, the Northeast Harbor innkeeper moved swiftly. He wanted to preserve the great landscape gardener's living legacy and create a public garden that distinguished his island town. As a prominent civic leader, Savage had often served as liaison between the summer colony and the year-round community on joint projects and in such local institutions as the Mount Desert Larger Parish. It was in this role that he and John D. Rockefeller Jr. (1874-1960) met and developed close ties.

On the surface, Rockefeller and Savage would seem to have little in common. Yet the son of America's first billionaire and the Northeast Harbor innkeeper both put aside personal aspirations to run their family enterprises. Given the choice, the two men may have taken similar paths, for they shared a talent and deep interest in landscape design and craftsmanship.

Savage had watched the construction of Acadia National Park's fifty-seven miles of carriage roads—among JDR, Jr.'s life works—for much of his

Robert W. Patterson, 1984.

LEFT: *Reef Point estate, circa 1950.*

youth. Savage marveled at how the design of the roads, stone bridges and gate houses blended with the landscape, subtly revealing natural features. He deeply appreciated that the carriage roads, built between 1913 and 1940, enabled the public to explore Mount Desert Island without trampling its wild, fragile beauty.

In the early 1950s, JDR, Jr. and Savage corresponded frequently about various land transactions in Northeast Harbor. These two men also shared a passion for Asian art in its many forms—from Japanese porcelain to Chinese bronzes. Their letters reveal a warm friendship and mutual admiration. "Our association throughout the years has been a pleasant one. That fact and the further fact that it has grown closer with the mounting years is undoubtedly due to our having common interests, tastes and ideals," Rockefeller wrote to Charles Savage in 1955. "We have long worked together in various matters affecting the well-being of the island. That our association has become closer of late and that we have so much in common is to me a happy circumstance. On various occasions, I have endeavored to have you know in what high regard and friendship I hold you. That you think of me in such kindly terms is heart-warming."

Savage had seen and admired Rockefeller's own Farrand garden atop Barr Hill. Seeking to preserve Farrand's wealth of plantings, Savage turned to the elderly philanthropist for assistance. Though the innkeeper had already bought the extensive plant material, the purchase did not cover its costly removal from the Reef Point estate, a task he had less than a year to complete.

In an exchange of letters with Rockefeller starting in 1956, Savage outlined plans to move the Reef Point collection to Northeast Harbor, where the plantings would be used to embellish the Thuya

LEFT: *Paths, stone and water: Some of the many 'faces' of the Asticou Azalea Garden.*

Lodge grounds, part of the Asticou Terraces Trust left to the Town of Mount Desert by summer resident Joseph Henry Curtis. Savage had known the Boston landscape architect well as a neighbor and proprietor of the Asticou Inn. Upon Curtis' death in 1928, Savage was appointed the first trustee to oversee the property and continued in this role until the mid 1960s.

But Savage felt that Farrand's extensive and unusual collection of azaleas warranted its own garden, with greater visibility than the more hidden Asticou Terraces afforded. To showcase Farrand's prize azalea and rhododendron collection, he proposed creating a roadside garden on his own property west of the Asticou Inn. Savage saw the landscaping project as raising Northeast Harbor's profile as a vacation destination for yachtsmen and discriminating visitors, and as a means of transforming an unsightly swamp area.

"I firmly believe that we shall both be very pleased and satisfied at the results," the innkeeper wrote to Rockefeller in the late spring of 1956. "While it has been appreciated as located in the Bar Harbor garden, the specimens have occupied a rather cramped site there. Here, the enlarged acreage, varied terrain and happy circumstance of water will permit vastly broadened effects of display."

A SHARED VISION

JDR, Jr. not only endorsed Savage's vision to save their friend's Reef Point collection, but pledged his monetary support to finance the initial execution of what would one day become the Thuya and Asticou Azalea gardens. Aesthetically, the two men saw eye-to-eye, holding the preservation of Mount Desert's beauty uppermost.

With only a year to extract Farrand's vast plant collection, Savage dispatched his sixteen-year-old

Savage patron and friend, John D. Rockefeller, Jr., shown here at his Seal Harbor estate with son, Winthrop.

Rhododendron yedoense var. poukhanense

Flourishing Korean azalea near the Sand Garden.

"I drew boxes and then labeled the box with the name of the plant, having filled in the color to match the plant as best I could," remembers Mary Ann Savage Habib, a Smith College graduate who was home that summer from Abbot Academy in Andover, Massachusetts. "This involved several trips over there as the azaleas varied in when they bloomed."

Savage's valued foreman was Arthur "Mike" Coombs, who had earlier worked for estate gardener Philip McLean. In his blue Ford truck with its flatbed trailer, Coombs often made up to two trips daily to Farrand's estate to dig up and remove the Reef Point plant

daughter, Mary Ann, to Reef Point, where she used colored pencils to make swatches of each of the azalea's hues as the blossoms emerged. She made repeated trips to create the color chart and bloom calendar. This greatly enhanced her father's ability to determine where the Kyushu, roseshell and other azaleas would be replanted and to incorporate the bloom sequence in his design for the garden.

material to Northeast Harbor. An affable, unflappable man who usually had a pipe clamped between his teeth, Coombs and his crew did the backbreaking job of carefully unearthing the azaleas, rhododendrons and other shrubs and perennials. A Boston firm came up with an extra-large truck to extract the Sargent weeping hemlock, Alberta spruces and other trees.

Gary Tyler, custodian of the Mount Desert public school for decades, was among the hard-working islanders who assisted Coombs. Tyler, who would later serve as a gardener at Thuya Garden, has vivid memories of the Reef Point Gardens. "It was the first time I had ever seen white straw-berries." Tyler recalled. "They came, I believe, from France."

Like a painter's preliminary sketch, the Azalea Garden's bones were roughed out in broad strokes that summer. Black-and-white photos of the first efforts, no doubt taken by the landscape designer for posterity and his patron's review, show a gouged-out gully and crudely shaped pond.

Savage knew the strong work ethic and fine craftsmanship of the island people and turned to Northeast Harbor contractor Maurice Burr to ex-cavate the fire pond and alder swamp just west of the Asticou Inn. Luckily, the fall of 1956 was mild, allowing Burr and crew to fill the swampy area, covering it with a topsoil of sandy loam before the ground froze. They also bolstered the banks of the stream flowing through the Azalea Garden with fieldstones and boulders. Quarryman Joe Musetti and Savage spent hours in Hall Quarry looking for the perfect pitch pine to provide a focal point for the planned sand garden.

Clad in insulated coveralls, Coombs, Burr, Austin Gott, Herb Strout and Tyler labored through Christmas and into the new year, despite a blan-

SERVING THE VISION

Arthur Fennelly Coombs (1910-1999), known as Mike, had a literal hand in the creation of both the Asticou Azalea and Thuya gardens. Quite simply, Charles Savage's life's works would not have come to be or survived so well over half a century without the tireless labor, gardening exper-tise and unwavering devotion of this collaborator from Northeast Harbor.

Coombs was an outdoorsman who loved to fish, hunt and camp. He made gardening his livelihood, learning such essential horticultural skills as how to amend soil, prune properly, deadhead spent blossoms and plant bare-root trees and shrubs from elder estate gardener Philip Mclean. As part of the crew tending Philadelphia sculptor Agnes Yarnall LePage's Somes Sound garden and other estates in Northeast Harbor, Coombs learned to garden from McLean, who came from Cape Breton Island and lived with his sister Annie in Northeast Harbor.

As the Asticou Terraces Trust's sole trustee, Savage turned to Coombs in 1945 to supervise the upkeep of Thuya Lodge and the shelters, lookouts and walking paths criss-crossing Asticou Hill. The innkeeper entrusted Coombs with the laborious retrieval of Beatrix Farrand's botanical collection from her Reef Point estate in Bar Harbor and the execution and maintenance of both the Asticou Azalea and Thuya gardens starting in 1957.

After retiring in 1974, Coombs still lived by the rhythms of the garden. He kept his considerable green thumb firmly in the dirt, growing Farrand's hardy azaleas, as well as perennials and annuals, at his small nursery, The Flower Pot, in Northeast Harbor. He and his wife Marguerite eventually moved to Longwood, Florida, to be closer to their children and grandchildren.

ket of snow. More black-and-white snapshots show the crew trundling wrapped shrubs in an old wooden wheelbarrow and setting the great slab of Somes Sound granite to form the first of the Azalea Garden's two footbridges spanning the stream.

EAST MEETS MAINE

Initially, the Azalea Garden was conceived as a drive-by display to be viewed entirely from

1917, at the Museum of Fine Arts in Boston. And he traveled to the Brooklyn Botanic Garden in New York to visit the Japanese Hill-and-Pond Garden, America's first public Japanese garden.

Savage recognized the parallels between the Maine and Japanese landscapes. "It is a significant fact that many features of the natural scenery of Mount Desert have similarities to the Japanese, particularly in the parts of the island where bold

Pitch pine often called "natural bonsai," growing amidst the granite ledges near Sand Beach.

CENTER: *Artful planting of R. 'Mary Fleming' alongside one of the island's lichen-flecked boulders.*

RIGHT: *Main bridge constructed by Joe Musetti.*

Peabody Drive. But as the reflecting pond took shape, Japan, where garden design is an ancient art form, increasingly became a source of ideas and inspiration. Savage procured books and pored over pictures and descriptions of Kyoto's Katsura Imperial Gardens and the famed Zen rock garden at the Ryoan-ji Temple. He consulted with Patterson, Maine's first registered landscape architect. He visited Tenshin-en (Garden of the Heart of Heaven), a Japanese rock garden dating from

ledges, rocks and pitch pine prevail," Savage wrote in 1957. "From the outset, it appeared that to the water and azaleas there ought to be added certain accents in the form of rocks. It was but a further step to add pines."

He went to great lengths to find fine things that caught his eye. He combed Maine beaches and regarded the smooth, rounded cobbles and other rocks as gems. He especially prized small, polished sedimentary pebbles striped in red, brown and black from a remote beach in Washington County. A crew was sent to haul a truckload of these beach stones from Jasper Beach in Bucks Harbor. With the Katsura Imperial Garden's rocky shore in mind, he created a peninsula of pebbles in the Azalea Garden.

As the alders were cleared, the swamp's inner reaches proved far more extensive than earlier thought. The landscape design was broadened to include a second reflecting pool. Farther inland, distant spruce forests were incorporated, and cedars, hemlocks and pitch pines planted to form an evergreen curtain. A stately American larch still remains a major design element in this section of the garden. "These evergreen trees form the background for the arrangements of azalea shrubs," commented Savage. "The foreground is that of the water."

As areas of wetland were filled, a flat expanse emerged on the eastern edge of the property. Having seen photos of the famed Zen rock garden at Kyoto's Ryoan-ji Temple, Savage set about creating his own dry landscape. First, a low wall was built with flat, black stone slabs salvaged from the terraces at Kenarden Lodge that had been created for railroad king John S. Kennedy on Bar Harbor's Shore Path. Brilliant red roof tiles retrieved from the demolished Fabbri family's Bar Harbor villa, Buonriposo, were artfully woven between the slabs to provide a decorative touch.

JOE'S QUARRY

Joseph P. Musetti (1920-2005), the last quarryman to extract stone commercially on Mount Desert Island, had a hand in the Asticou Azalea Garden. The Italian-American, whose family still lives in the village of Hall Quarry, overlooking Somes Sound, quarried and shaped the grey granite slab and other rough-cut stones for the garden's main bridge in 1956, with the help of his right-hand man, Delmont Lanpher.

Musetti, whose parents Amelio and Adele Musetti emigrated from Italy to the United States in the late nineteenth century, traced his ancestry back to the hillside village of Giovagallo in northern Tuscany. The region, Massa Carrara, is famous for its pure white marble favored by sculptors from Michelangelo to Henry Moore. His forebears were among the Italian immigrants whose stone-cutting skills were much in demand starting in the nineteenth century in the United States. Many of these immigrants came to Maine, which had become the nation's top granite producer in value of quarried stone by the early twentieth century. Musetti operated his quarry on the western shore of Somes Sound, an area known for fine-grained, pink flecked stone.

In 1929, Musetti quarried, cut and laid the stone for the triple-arched Duck Brook Bridge, with its corbelled viewing platforms. His granite and craftsmanship is also visible at St. Peter's Roman Catholic Church in the Southwest Harbor village of Manset and in numerous stone walls thoughout the island.

In later years, Musetti and his son Ron would drive by the Asticou Azalea Garden and the Duck Brook Bridge so the elder man could see his handiwork. "He wouldn't say anything," Ronald Musetti said. "Just point."

R. 'Olga Mezitt'

ABOVE RIGHT: *Granite bench with* Malus floribunda, *Japanese flowering crabapple.*

OPPOSITE: *Early bloom, mid-May, Japanese cherry tree.*

For the sand, Savage considered the hue and grain size of various samples before choosing a fine, white quartz sand from a West Virginia quarry that was shipped by boxcar to the Ellsworth railroad station. The silica sand was then spread in this flat oblong area of the garden. The composition was completed when a dozen lichen-flecked boulders were carefully placed to stand like islands in the flat white expanse.

These boulders had been located the previous fall by Savage, who combed Asticou Hill in search of aged rocks that suggested Mount Desert Island's unique rugged beauty and character. That winter, unobstructed by vegetation, his crew used crowbars, rollers and sleds to extract and haul the assortment of worn, weathered granite from the icy ledges and snowy woods.

To heighten the garden's effect, Savage created special wooden rakes with widely spaced teeth and showed the workmen how to rake the fine sand in patterns resembling the rhythmic motion of waves. Not everyone took to the Zen practice. "I had one man who quit on me," recalled Tyler, chuckling. "I said to the gentleman, 'You know if you kind of walked flat-footed, it would be much easier to get your grooves in there.' He replied, 'Nobody is going to tell me how to walk.' He went up to the shop, picked up his rubber boots and away he went."[8]

Come summer, Tyler and Les Sherer had the job of unearthing lambkill, Labrador tea and other native plants from the Great Heath, a vast peat bog in Bar Harbor. The scene was straight out of *The African Queen.* "It was so hot, we got right down to our underwear. We had Moxie [a unique Maine soda pop]," Tyler said. "We'd go in with an old axe and cut this stuff out and then we'd come back and plant it."[9]

By the spring of 1958, the Azalea Garden was blooming. Through Savage's camera lens, the crudely sketched composition visible in the early photographs had been replaced by a subtly rendered watercolor. In the foreground, viewers gaze through a fine veil of pale pink blossoms. The sweet, snow and swamp azaleas are complemented and enhanced by cherry and crabapple blossoms. The flowering masses have the delicacy of filigree lace. Great mounds of rose, salmon, light pink and other pastel-hued shrubs bask in the spring sun. Greenery and blurred patches of color are mirrored in the pond's clear waters.

Rockefeller was pleased and communicated his pleasure to Charles Savage enthusiastically. "May I assure you again that I am delighted to have been your silent partner in this matter," JDR, Jr. wrote in a September 2, 1957 letter from The Eyrie. "What you have already accomplished is charming and most rewarding."

That summer, while the garden was still under construction, motorists were already slowing down to take in the scene. To Savage's great pleasure, the observers included area workers as well as tourists and summer visitors. "One of the most rewarding sights for the designer has been the fact that at 7 o'clock in the morning and again at 3:30 in the afternoon, almost all of the workmen who drive to or from their work have been observed to stop for a few moments in passing," Savage wrote

Rhododendron kiusianum

Kyushu azaleas lining the stream with Sargent weeping hemlock transplanted in 1957 from Reef Point.

in a 1958 report tracing the Azalea Garden's history. "Some have regularly come back later with their wives."[10]

As Savage had hoped, the Azalea Garden not only enhanced the Asticou Inn but the whole village, in all seasons. In the fall, his roadside painting assumed a fresh palette with gold, sienna, scarlet and other vibrant colors reflected in the pond. Come winter, the snow-wreathed pitch pine and other evergreens took center stage while the pond became the neighborhood ice rink. A good skater himself, Savage joined in the fun while his wife Katharine provided cookies and hot chocolate for the crowd.

"You must be told how often people speak to me of the beauty of your plantation," Eleanor Belmont, a summer resident and patron of the arts, wrote to the innkeeper in 1957. "Perhaps more than this, [though, is] the humility with which it has been done, the great taste, and the generosity of your public spirit which has made so great a contribution to Northeast Harbor and its charm."

ties made it seem staid, passé to the new generation of vacationers.

Then, in May 1960, John D. Rockefeller, Jr. died. Two years later, Savage's brother George, who had studied at Harvard under famed twentieth-century architect and Bauhaus founder Walter Gropius, died of a sudden heart attack just as his architectural practice was starting to flourish.

CHANGING TIMES

But even as Savage's garden was taking its place in the hearts of visitors and residents alike, his very livelihood, the Asticou Inn, was floundering. American's lifestyles had dramatically changed. In Northeast Harbor, as elsewhere on the Maine coast, stately inns that had survived on repeat clientele were in trouble. Their valued customers were dying and their customers' children were not taking their place. The Asticou's no-liquor policy, absence of a swimming pool and other old-fashioned quali-

Savage struggled to keep the inn afloat, but mounting debts, dwindling revenue and under-capitalization pushed the Asticou Inn into financial collapse. In 1964, Asti-Kim, a corporation of summer residents including Rockefeller's son David, acquired the Savage family's foreclosed business from the bank. While introducing some change, Asti-Kim has strived to retain the establishment's old-fashioned charm.

The 1960s were likely a disappointing period in Savage's life, but his wife, children, and extended

family gave him great pleasure and support. "I never saw him get angry at anything. He might have, but I never saw it. There were plenty of times that he could have," recalled Don Coates, who worked closely with the innkeeper for decades and still serves on the Mount Desert Land & Garden Preserve Board. "He used to get in his car and he'd ride and calm himself down if he had a problem. Or he'd go to the studio and play his piano."

Savage continued to contribute to his community through the Village Improvement Society, undertaking landscaping projects to enhance the dramatic views along Sargeant Drive and the Neighborhood House. He also did some private landscape design for various estates in town and later co-taught a landscape design class at College of the Atlantic.

In 1966, following the lead of Joseph Curtis, who generously left the Asticou Terraces Trust to the inhabitants of the Town of Mount Desert and its summer residents in the 1920s, Savage gave the Asticou Azalea Garden to the town. From the very beginning, he had conceived of both the Asticou Azalea and Thuya gardens as special features distinguishing his hometown from other coastal Maine communities. He wanted to be sure the public and local residents would have the opportunity to enjoy them in perpetuity.

Although the Azalea Garden lacked its own endowment, which the Thuya Garden had, Savage's living treasure was put in good hands. At about the same time as this transfer was happening, Acadia National Park's chief naturalist, Paul G. Favour, Jr., was appointed trustee of the Asticou Terraces Trust established by Curtis. The trust was contracted by the town to care for the Azalea Garden, and Favour's head gardener "Mike" Coombs and crew—the men who had labored to build both the Azalea and Thuya gardens—took over the care of both gardens.

AN ENDURING VISION

Favour, who had made Northeast Harbor his permanent home after retiring from the Park Service, was well qualified to safeguard Savage's horticultural creations. As Acadia's top naturalist, it was his job to know Mount Desert Island's flora and fauna intimately—and he did. He could spot and identify the shrubby cinquefoil, dainty grass-pink orchid, insect-eating round-leafed sundew and a wealth of other plants growing wild on the Maine isle, with one glance. He understood Savage's artful mingling of native and exotic species in the Azalea Garden and the conditions the plants required to thrive and look their best.

Rhododendron 'mucronatum'

A friendly, down-to-earth person, Favour shared his knowledge and educated others without being patronizing. The park ranger was not a gardener, but he had Mike Coombs and then the head gardener's equally capable, good-natured successor, Tim Taylor, to guide him and see to the

BEATRIX FARRAND'S CHERRY TREE

Each spring for over half a century, the Asticou Azalea Garden's Japanese cherry tree has put on a heady show for all the senses. Its display is every bit as lovely as the famed Yoshino cherry trees in Washington, D.C., yet it thrives in the coastal Maine climate.

"A magical cloud of pink blossoms," is how Mary Roper, Azalea Garden manager, has described it. The effect is heightened by hordes of hummingbirds flitting between the blossoms and filling the air with their high-pitched sound.

"The tree's exceptional nature and beauty must have already been apparent when Mr. Savage planted it at the Azalea Garden, because he gave the tree a very prominent spot," she added.

A hybrid species, finely textured and densely branched, the Japanese cherry blooms profusely for up to five days. The tree is thought to have originated at the Arnold Arboretum in Jamaica Plain, Massachusetts. As a natural seedling, it was likely shipped to American garden designer Beatrix Farrand for a colder climate trial at her Reef Point Gardens in Bar Harbor. In 1957, the tree was moved with other precious plantings to Northeast Harbor.

Recently, Farrand's cherry tree has begun to decline. Cuttings have been taken and are being propagated in the hopes of recreating the genetically unique tree and ensuring the springtime ritual for another half century. "We would welcome another fifty years of bloom," Roper said.

Azalea Garden's upkeep for eighteen years. Savage, who lived in Clover Cottage, just a stone's throw away, also continued to keep a close eye on things. In his subtle way, the garden's creator would drop a gentle hint when a certain pine needed pruning or a flowering shrub could use thinning.

Moss garden in the fall with royal azalea in yellow fall color.

OPPOSITE PAGE:
Curving entrance path into the Asticou Azalea Garden.

Grappling with an aging public sewer system, road reconstruction and other major municipal issues, Mount Desert officials decided in the early 1970s that the Azalea Garden deserved greater attention than the town could provide. They relinquished ownership of the living treasure and entrusted its future to the Mount Desert Land & Garden Preserve. In 1971, JDR, Jr.'s youngest son,

David, and his wife, Peggy, had established the nonprofit organization as a future repository for some of their Maine land holdings. The Azalea Garden was brought into its fold with the caveat that it be open to the public, as always intended.

In 1979, Savage died of a sudden heart attack on his way to Mount Desert Island Hospital in Bar Harbor. Shortly thereafter, his Japanese-inspired horticultural legacy got a new lease on life thanks to the generosity of Mary Clark Rockefeller (1938-1999). "Tod," as the first wife of Nelson A. Rockefeller was fondly called by family and friends, summered her entire life in Northeast Harbor. The tall, witty outdoorswoman was happiest tramping through the woods looking for the rose-hued arethusa orchid and other wild botanical rarities on Mt. Desert Island. She also enjoyed working in her own gardens under an immense sun hat. Marion Rockefeller Weber, a niece, remembered seeking her aunt out, "while she knelt at work in her gardens, to ask her questions and wait for the amusing replies to float up like bubbles from under the voluminous sunbonnet."

Tod Rockefeller had known Savage for years. They both possessed a passion for native plants and enjoyed many related exchanges. Savage carved the surviving sign leading to her family's shingle-style cottage, Seaward. After his death, she gave $50,000 to the Azalea Garden to honor the landscape designer and pay tribute to her late former

father-in-law. She and JDR, Jr. had remained close and held similar conservation ethics. Without his financial backing, she knew, the garden would not have been created.

By the 1980s, the Land & Garden Preserve had established the Asticou Azalea Garden Committee. Elise F. Hawtin, whose colonial-style cottage, Harbor Head, overlooked the Great Pond, was the first chair. Hawtin was the daughter of longtime Northeast Harbor summer resident, Gertrude Fay, a petite woman who climbed one of the Mount Desert hills almost daily well into her

eighties. Fay was close to the Savage family, having spent thirty summers in their home as a paying guest.

Hawtin kept watch over the Azalea Garden. She could clearly see that the Great Pond and smaller Lily Pond needed dredging. Silt had built up on the bottom and invasive duckweed and bulrushes were encroaching on the two pools, altering their ecosystems. As the Azalea Garden committee's chair, she consulted Patterson, who recommended using the Mary C. Rockefeller Azalea Garden Fund to dredge both ponds as part

Consummate host and gentleman, Charles K. Savage welcomed guests fireside as manager of the historic Jordan Pond house, circa 1970.

of a broader landscape design plan that established a proper entrance and parking area and linked the path system in the garden to provide a continuous loop that would accommodate the growing number of visitors.

For the actual design, Patterson recommended Patrick Chassé, who was a Harvard graduate student in landscape architecture. Chassé, born in northern Maine's Aroostook County, now serves as the first landscape curator at the venerable Isabella Stewart Gardner Museum in Boston. He was the founding president of the Beatrix Farrand Society. Chassé had discovered the Azalea Garden and met Savage as a college student. Savage was among those who inspired him to pursue landscape design.

Chassé has said that Savage's fusion of Eastern and Western elements stands out in the Northeast. "He was perfectly comfortable with a foot in both worlds and he could make them work," he said. The Asticou Azalea Garden, added the landscape designer, makes people feel as though it were

their own. "It has a wonderful intimacy as you move through it."

Mindful of that flow, Chassé altered the garden's main entrance from a private residence's lawn opposite the Asticou Inn to Route 198, where a discreet gravel driveway and parking area were constructed. To mark the entrance, a silvered-wood fence was built, along with a roofed gate, Japanese-style, supported by pillars. Passing through the gate, visitors find themselves in an enchanting forest chamber, welcomed by a sea of emerald-green moss, interspersed with lush ferns.

At the sand garden, Chassé repeated Savage's clay-tile pattern to set apart the white silica sand from the pink granite stone dust covering the walkway. Bunchberry and wintergreen, interwoven among the tiles, soften the effect. In the brook, the designer added a series of stepping stones, inviting visitors to diverge from the paths, in order to chance upon the moss chapel or encounter the sand garden from a different direction.

After nearly two decades of service, Favour resigned his post at the Asticou Terraces Trust. Luckily, as the Great Pond's dredging got underway, the steadfast steward was succeeded by an equally dedicated man who knew both gardens very well. Don E. Coates, a Savage family friend, graciously accepted the town's appeal to replace Favour as trustee in 1984. Coates and his wife, Alida, had come to Northeast Harbor in 1946. He taught at the former Gilman High School, and was principal at Mount Desert High School for a decade. Summers, Coates worked as Savage's associate overseeing the bookkeeping for the Asticou Inn, Acadia Corporation and Asticou Terraces Trust.

Pincushion moss and granite Nomen style lantern.

LEFT: *Main entrance.*

FAR LEFT: *Stepping stones and* Rhododendron yedoense var. poukhanense.

Granite bench in the Sand Garden Overlook facing toward the east.

RIGHT: *Mugo pines along the roadside, a design feature introduced to the garden by Tom Hall, inspired by the mountains of Mount Desert.*

At the Azalea Garden, Don Coates inherited the dredging project. Previous attempts to pump the built-up silt and sludge from the lily pond had failed. The career educator tackled the problem by hiring some able-bodied, unemployed workers from Ellsworth who were willing to manually deepen the pond. Coates also attacked the root cause of the sedimentation further upstream by finding federal funding to create a series of settling basins designed to reduce the flow of silt into the ponds. For his special efforts and the innovative engineering work involved, Don Coates received an award from the United States Department of Agriculture, Soil Conservation Services.

Coates was also instrumental in hiring the Azalea Garden's first fulltime gardener, Amy Davis. This freed Thuya superintendent Tim Taylor and his crew to focus more of their energies on Thuya Garden, Thuya Lodge and the extensive trail system on Asticou Hill.

PASSIONATE STEWARDSHIP

Gardens are labor intensive and expensive to maintain and rapidly fade without proper care and vision. Unlike Great Britain, where historic gardens are treated as living treasures, the United States has lagged behind in its commitment to historic landscape preservation. Fortunately for the Azalea Garden, passionate stewards have stepped forward.

In the early spring of 1986, Thomas S. Hall (1909-1990) took over from Hawtin as the Azalea committee chair. Hall, who summered for years in Northeast Harbor, had served as a dean at Washington University in St. Louis, where he taught biology and zoology. He brought passion, boundless energy and good humor to all his work, from the Missouri Botanical Garden to Bar Harbor's College of the Atlantic. His enthusiasm had a way of firing the imagination of others.

Blessed with a deep love of plants and gardens, Hall applied his intellect and creativity to the Azalea Garden as though it were his own. As

he saw it, the azaleas and rhododendrons needed greater grooming. Wild blackberry and other invasive native shrubs had sprung up: Everything needed a haircut.

Hall's own Maine garden, with its series of shaped mugo pines suggesting the wavelike Mount Desert hills flowing down toward the shore, had been partly inspired by a great Japanese garden—the moss garden at the Saiho-ji Temple in Kyoto. His tenure as committee chair saw an enhancement and expansion of the Japanese nature of the Azalea Garden. He brought in two Japanese landscape architects who taught him and the garden staff how to properly prune, thin and shape shrubs and trees. Several Japanese rough-hewn stone lanterns crafted in the Kasuga and Nomen style and four found-stone granite benches were procured

and placed around the garden to accent particular areas and views. Since all the tags identifying Farrand's original azaleas from Reef Point either had been lost or stolen, the process of pinpointing the several dozen varieties was begun, with help from azalea expert Fred Galle.

Most of all, Hall will be remembered for his bold vision to landscape the finger of land separating the highway from the reflecting pond. To soften the flat visual line and shield the garden from vehicular traffic, he had a series of mugo pine trees planted on the eastern end. These pines are pruned, or candled, annually to retain the rounded, flowing forms that resemble the undulating mountains of Mount Desert. The altered roadside view had its critics, but the mountain motif has gradually become an intrinsic part of the Azalea Garden.

Tom Hall enjoying the warm fall colors on the east lawn in 1988.

LEFT: *Granite bench in the Sand Garden Overlook facing toward the west.*

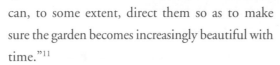

Poetic Kasuga-style granite lantern with royal azalea.

RIGHT: *Mary Roper, Garden Manager, and Beth Straus, honorary Asticou Azalea Garden committee chair, have been a creative and aesthetic team since 1990.*

FAR RIGHT: *The curving east lawn path as viewed from the crabapple arch.*

Change comes hard in beloved gardens, Thomas Hall once remarked, but it is truly inevitable in gardens composed mainly of trees and shrubs. "Charles Savage planted copses of pitch pine and hemlocks that were about six feet in height. Today, they are forty feet high. The streams and pools that Savage created are constantly reshaping themselves. The rhododendrons and laurels have quadrupled in height as Charles Savage knew, and indeed, hoped that they would. We cannot prevent these changes. We must accept and respect them. But we can, to some extent, direct them so as to make sure the garden becomes increasingly beautiful with time."[11]

Sadly, just four years after he took on the Azalea Garden, in the spring of 1990, Hall died of a massive heart attack. He would have been a hard act to follow had his successor not possessed the same sharp mind as Hall and shared his deep interest and knowledge in visual art and Japanese garden design.

Like Savage, Beth Straus, who took charge of the Azalea Garden Committee after Hall died, grew up by the sea. They shared, too, the experience of living on an island. Hers was Belvedere in San Francisco Bay. The family lived many summers on the steep-sided island where the air is scented with wild freesia and nasturtiums. Victorian cottages with vertical gardens overflowing with roses, camellias, gardenias and other flowers, flank the limestone cliffs. Winters were spent in a house perched on a cliff overlooking the Pacific Ocean.

"I had a beautiful room with cream-colored walls and a big window opening right out to the sea. You could look out and see the ships coming in, the surf on the beach, and the waves rolling out to a lighthouse that flashed off and on at night," wrote Straus, recalling her San Francisco home in a 2005 memoir. "The windows swung out, and when there was a storm my mother tied the window to my bedpost to keep it from being blown off. It tugged and tugged and tugged at me all night

long while the waves boomed under the house. As the wind tugged, the lighthouses of San Francisco would go on and off on my wall, each with their own rhythm of light."[12]

Growing up in San Francisco, Straus acquired an affinity for the rich Asian culture and traditions, whether it was Chinese pastries, fine Japanese porcelain or the silk and cotton kimonos that women wore as dressing gowns. In later years, she traveled in Japan, leading the Museum of Modern Art's International Council on a trip that included Kyoto's famed garden, Ryoan-ji, where moss-covered boulders stand in a sea of white sand raked in wave patterns.

Rhododendron kaempfari

The serene Sand Garden with torch azalea in bloom.

OPPOSITE: *Cindy Robbins, Bonsai master Yuji Yoshimura, Beth Straus, and Mary Roper in 1992.*

Straus began working with Hall in the Azalea Garden while her husband served with him on the board of trustees of College of the Atlantic, located in Bar Harbor. Together, Hall and Straus hired the 1985 College of the Atlantic graduate Mary Roper as the Azalea Garden manager. At the time, Roper was working for a local plantsman and had conferred previously with Hall in his capacity as the college's board chair.

When Amy Davis left as head gardener, recalled Roper, "Tom Hall called me up one morning and said, 'Would you like to be head muckety-muck?' and wasn't he right!" Her lofty job ranges from cloud-pruning the Scotch pines to digging silt out from the brook and ponds.

Coming to Maine in the 1970s as guests of their close friends David and Peggy Rockefeller, Straus visited the Azalea Garden and felt right at home. "I always felt close to Japanese things," she has said. Straus and her late husband, Don, eventually bought a white clapboard house in the Mount Desert village of Somesville, where a sweeping view of Somes Sound and Sargent Mountain could be seen from their back porch. They loved the island and made it their permanent home.

Roper, an Alabama native whose family's passion was hunting for pyrite, marcasite, amazonite and other minerals, fell in love with the Azalea Garden, where aged granite rocks are revered as much as the plantings. Moved by the story of

Savage's eleventh-hour rescue of Farrand's botanical collection, she makes every effort to showcase his genius and carry on his vision.

Throughout this endeavor, Straus has served as mentor and collaborator. A magna cum laude Stanford graduate, Straus nurtured Roper's horticultural skills and talent in landscape design. As the Azalea Garden's chair, she enabled the garden manager to attend the first International Japanese Garden Symposium in Portland, Oregon and to attend an intensive seminar in Japan to study other gardens, including Kyoto's Ryoan-ji and Katsura Imperial Villa, the gardens that had so inspired Savage.

Straus, who was vice president of the New York Botanical Garden and spearheaded the revival of Farrand's forgotten rose garden there in the mid-1980s, also made it possible for Japanese bonsai master Yuji Yoshimura to do extensive pruning in the Azalea Garden and to instruct Roper and her staff. Ivan Watters, bonsai curator at the Chicago Botanic Garden, has assumed this work in more recent years.

Like Savage, Straus' greatest gift has been her unerring eye. A finely tuned sense of symmetry and spatial relationships—proportion and harmony—has enabled her to pinpoint and excise a flaw or imbalance at a glance. Her light touch and clarity of composition is manifest throughout the Azalea Garden. "Her demeanor—her presence—

pointed toward refinement," Roper reflected. "She might come to the garden and say, 'We don't really need that tree,' and she would be right."

CONTEMPLATIVE SPACE

As the Asticou Azalea Garden came into its own, the colonial-style cottage that overlooked the Great Pond became increasingly at odds with the Japanese-inspired landscape design. Harbor Head, the century-old house that had once served as the village post office, occupied Pedder's Corner where Route 198 and Peabody Drive meet. Up until 2004, the cottage had been the residence of the Asticou Garden Committee's first chair, Elise F. Hawtin.

In 2004, following the former chair's death, the Mount Desert Land & Garden Preserve made the decision to acquire Harbor Head from the Hawtin estate. Board members boldly decided to remove the building from the 1.2-acre parcel adjoining the Azalea Garden. In the Savage spirit, loath to discard anything reusable, workmen carefully took apart the three-story structure. Much of the building's material found new life in other homes.

The act of acquiring the Harbor Head property and removing all but a small wing of the house enabled the Azalea Garden's stewards to more fully buffer the horticultural jewel from two busy state highways. The land acquisition also included a grassy pathway, providing westerly access to the Great Pond. In 2007, this new access made it possible for heavy machinery to be brought in, with minimal damage, to extract excess silt from the reflecting pools. Every decade or so, the pond will need to be dredged to maintain its depth, water quality and health.

"We are once again amazed that our practical needs are steering us in the right direction," Roper said. "They are fitting into the aesthetic framework." The decision to tear down Harbor Head took vision and much thought. But by eliminating the house, the Azalea Garden has gained greater space and light to breathe.

In a moving remembrance, Roper recently recounted: "Beth has said, 'the greater the challenge, the more opportunity we have to be ourselves.' It's about meeting the need for change with a strength and uniqueness that retains the spirit of the place. I think Beth has been very good at letting the garden become itself."

Today, entering the garden from the parking area, visitors still follow the crushed granite path through the moss corridor. Emerging from that green oasis, they have the option to turn west along a quiet meandering path. There, they'll encounter a 150-year-old russet apple tree and stroll along a seasonal stream where pinkshell azaleas (*Rhododen-*

dron vaseyi), native to the Blue Ridge Mountains of North Carolina, put on a subtle show in early spring. The spidery, rose-pink flowers tipped with cream-white from Farrand's Reef Point estate, form an integral part of the garden's structure.

Continuing west, where a small wing of the Harbor Head cottage remains, an evolving landscape unfolds. As the land slowly slopes upward, a series of asymmetrical hills swing into view. These gradually sloping berms, accented by a few pitch pine and weathered pink granite stones, resemble the undulating Mount Desert hills when seen from afar. Norumbega Mountain, looming in the distance, serves as a fitting backdrop.

In coming years, visitors strolling along the gently curving path will admire masses of low-lying azaleas planted among the softly contoured hillocks that serve as a sound barrier, and provide a visual treat for motorists and other passersby approaching the Pedder's Corner intersection. In this

The North Bridge with kurume, kyushu and flame azalea in bloom.

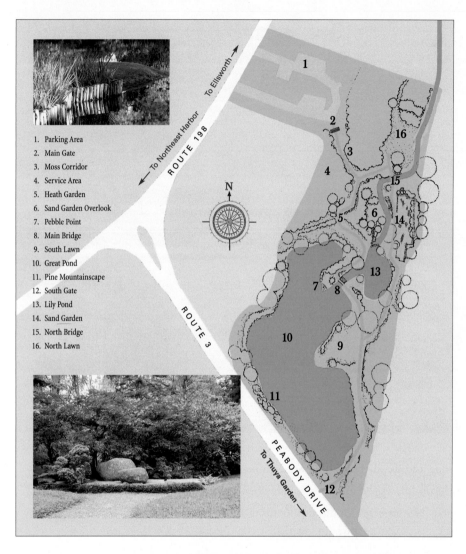

1. Parking Area
2. Main Gate
3. Moss Corridor
4. Service Area
5. Heath Garden
6. Sand Garden Overlook
7. Pebble Point
8. Main Bridge
9. South Lawn
10. Great Pond
11. Pine Mountainscape
12. South Gate
13. Lily Pond
14. Sand Garden
15. North Bridge
16. North Lawn

Map of the Asticou Azalea Garden. (Before 2008 expansion to the west of the Great Pond.)

airy place, not unlike a mountaintop, worn granite stepping stones lead down to the water's edge. A visitor can sit and view the old, partially submerged stones placed by Roper, or enjoy the sweeping vista across the Great Pond.

Taking her cue from Savage, Roper combed property owned by the Land & Garden Preserve on Asticou Hill in search of beautiful pink granite boulders whose lines, cracks and glacially-scoured surfaces conveyed the character and unique spirit of Mount Desert Island. Crew members worked through the late fall of 2007 to unearth the huge, totemic stone pieces using crowbars, rollers and wooden planks.

Many committed and caring people have had a hand in the western area's creation. The Quesada family contributed funds for much of the ongoing project through its Fore River Foundation to honor longtime Bar Harbor summer resident and Azalea Garden Committee member Kate Davis Quesada. David Slawson, a landscape designer who specializes in Japanese gardens, was consulted during the design phase.

Throughout, garden visitors now find a more restful quality. "The impression we have wanted to give is that the visitor is alone and able to have a personal experience and place for contemplation," Roper continued. "We just wanted to complete the feeling by creating as serene an environment as possible for the garden's many visitors."

LIVING LEGACY

Through the gentle coaxing of Straus, Roper and other devoted souls, the Azalea Garden finally has come into its own. Like a fine old wine, it has matured in time for its fiftieth birthday, celebrated throughout 2008. It's hard to imagine its creator wouldn't be pleased that the garden not only has survived, but has thrived, giving pleasure to the public, as intended. Surely, Charles Savage would be quietly gratified that his vision is being realized.

Finding his way to the Route 198 entrance, Savage would note the absence of a certain power pole and approve of the silvered cedar fence designed by his friend Robert Patterson. Stepping through the main gate, he undoubtedly would admire the pearl-necklace pattern made by the butt ends of hemlock branches protecting hair cap moss from foot traffic. He would also delight in Roper's artful east gate design, fashioned from white cedar and red maple twigs, conceived in the Savage and Craftsman spirit of reusing native material readily at hand.

Strolling along the crushed pink-granite path, Savage would emerge in the bright sunlight and see a towering white pine, its graceful boughs outstretched, greeting him like an old friend. Remembering the pitch pines gathered from the quarry when only four feet high, the designer would marvel at how the mountaintop character has emerged. Standing out in the pond's margins, the stockaded Japanese iris would be a welcome sight.

Though Savage would take pride in the Asticou Azalea Garden and its distinction in the garden world, he would have shied away from publicity unless it served a greater good. He would have steered attention to his distinguished mentors and collaborators, Farrand and Rockefeller. He would have recognized lesser-known, equally significant contributors, such as head gardeners Arthur "Mike" Coombs and Tim Taylor, faithful trustees Paul Favour and Don Coates, stonecutter Joe Musetti, and many others who had a literal hand either in the garden's creation or its survival.

Fresh hands continue the shaping. Roper and staff are expanding the Azalea Garden's western section in keeping with Savage's long-term land-

scape vision for the head of Northeast Harbor. Elise Felton, a Southwest Harbor resident and Azalea Garden Committee member, has put her horticultural expertise to work and has successfully grown from seed the now uncommon Kyushu, royal and pinkshell azaleas retrieved from Farrand's disassembled estate.

The current co-chairs of the Asticou Azalea Garden Committee, C.W. Eliot Paine and Jan Coates, have deep ties to the Savage family and the Azalea Garden. Paine is a descendent of A.C. Savage's early lodger and friend, Charles W. Eliot, who purchased property from the Savage family in 1880. He is now director emeritus of the Holden Arboretum in Kirtland, Ohio.

Jan Coates is Don Coates' youngest daughter. In 1999, following a career in higher education administration at Albion and Hamilton colleges, Jan Coates returned to Mount Desert Island full-time to assume ownership of the Port In A Storm Bookstore in Somesville. As a child, she often accompanied Coombs when he turned off the

water at the Azalea Garden at day's end. Savage, she said, used to light candles in Japanese lanterns arranged along the paths.

"It was a magical and mysterious place gently lighted by oblong Japanese lanterns on poles that playfully guided your walk through the garden," she remembers. "The sand garden fence has a shadow box near the top that was lit and provided a backdrop to the shapes, textures and contours of the sand garden under the night sky."

The Azalea Garden continues to weave a spell on all visitors, added Coates, whether they are year-round or seasonal sojourners of Mount Desert Island or brief visitors to Maine.

"The core design elements implemented by Charles Savage still guide and inspire the garden's development today," she reflected. "I believe Mr. Savage would be very proud of our stewardship and especially our efforts to honor the blending of East and West garden design with the natural beauty of the garden's stunning location. We look ahead to the next fifty years with enthusiasm."

END NOTES

1 Paula Deitz, *Beatrix Farrand: The Bulletins of Reef Point Gardens,* Sagapress, Inc., Sagaponack, NY, 1997. Available at the Northeast Harbor Library and for sale from the Mount Desert Land & Garden Preserve. $35.

2 Charles K. Savage, in an album tracing his creative work from 1918 to 1970. Available in the reference collection of the Northeast Harbor Library.

3 Robert Pyle, conversation with Letitia Baldwin, 2007.

4 Marcia Savage, in obituary for Katharine Larchar Savage, *Bar Harbor Times,* September, 2001.

5 Charles K. Savage, taped presentation to the Northeast Harbor Ladies Literary Club. 1974. Available to the public at the Northeast Harbor library.

6 IBID.

7 Robert W. Patterson, Farrand tribute, *Landscape Architecture,* American Society of Landscape Architects. 1959.

8 Gary Tyler, interview with Jan Coates, Mount Desert Land & Garden Preserve's co-chair, and Beth Straus, honorary chair. March 24, 2004. Taped interview available at the archives of the Mount Desert Land & Garden Preserve, Seal Harbor, Maine.

9 Harvesting wildflowers had been an accepted practice in the past, before concerns arose about protecting native species within their habitats, especially those growing within the fragile Mount Desert Island ecosystem.

10 Charles K. Savage, *Report to John D. Rockefeller, Jr.,* 1958. Text available at the archives of the Mount Desert Land & Garden Preserve, Seal Harbor, Maine.

11 Thomas S. Hall, Presentation to the Garden Club of Mount Desert, 1989. Text available at the archives of the Mount Desert Land & Garden Preserve, Seal Harbor, Maine.

12 Beth Straus, *Recollections,* a private memoir told to Donna Gold. Northern Light Press, Stockton Springs, ME. 2005.

PHOTOGRAPHY CREDITS

Legend: t/b (top/bottom) • l/r (left/right) • tl/tr (top left/top right) • bl/br/bc (bottom left/bottom right/bottom center) • c (center)

Jason Ashur pp 3, 26tr, 34l, 37l • Donald Brown p19r

Beatrix Farrand Society pp 16r, 18, 19 • Mary Greene pp 4, 17, 27, 28, 31r, 32, 40

John M. Hall pp cover, 6l, 7, 20tr, 22, 33l, 35, 39

Barbara Meyers p 41 • Rockefeller Family Archives p 21r

Mary Roper pp 2bl, 2bc, 2br, 3bl, 3br, 3bc, 5, 20tl, 21t, 24l, 24c, 24r, 26tl, 29l, 29c, 30tl, 30tr, 31l, 32, 34r, 36, 36r, 45tr, 45c, 45br, 47rt, 47rb

Alice H. Savage p 15r • Charles K. Savage pp 11r, 12r, 13r, 14r, 15t

©Robert Thayer Photography pp 6r, 10, 26tl, 38c, 42, 43, 46

ACKNOWLEDGMENTS

Many generous and knowing people have contributed their time, memories, documents, images, and memorabilia for use in the research and writing of the two books commemorating the 50th anniversary of the Asticou Azalea and Thuya Gardens. They include: Sandy Agrafiotis, Jessica Savage Anderson, Jason Ashur, Patrick Chassé, Don, Alida, and Jan Coates, the Crofoot family, Paula Deitz, Ruth Elkins, Donna Gold, John M. Hall, Lawrie Harris, Priscilla Hutton, Cathy Jewitt, Carl Kelley, Brenda Les, Robert Linnane, Phoebe Milliken, the Musetti family, Lee Patterson, Don Phillips, Robert Pyle, Todd Richardson, Mary Roper, Rose Ruze, C. Kenneth Savage, Jr., Mary Ann Savage Habib, Richard "Rick" Savage, Connie Seavey, Peggy Simpson, Beth Straus, Raymond Strout, Tim Taylor, Robert Thayer, Helen and Bill Townsend, and Gary Tyler.

Archives, institutions, and repositories that provided critical additional information for the garden books include: Acadia National Park, Arnold Arboretum of Harvard University, Bar Harbor Historical Society, Beatrix Farrand Society, College of the Atlantic, Down East Magazine Publishers, Greenrock Company, Jamaica Plain Historical Society, Jesup Memorial Library, Mount Auburn Cemetery Archives, Mount Desert Historical Society, Mount Desert Land & Garden Preserve, Noble and Greenough School, Northeast Harbor Library, Old House Interiors Publishers, Rockefeller Family Archives, Town of Mount Desert, and Waltham Historical Society.

We also wish to express special appreciation to those individuals who have provided critical encouragement and support of this effort from its inception. They include: Don Coates, Jan Coates, Heather Frazer, Betsy Hewlett, Ann Judd, C. W. Eliot Paine, Carole Plenty, Ken Savage, Mary Ann Savage Habib, Beth Straus, Rodman Ward, and members of the Board of Directors of the Mount Desert Land & Garden Preserve under the leadership of Neva Goodwin and its 50th Anniversary Committee chaired by Nancy Putnam.

Members of the Thuya Garden and Azalea Garden Committees have supported this effort through their generosity and attendance at meetings in the middle of beautiful Mount Desert summers. They are: Scott Asen, Kate Baxter, Sigrid Berwind, Patricia Blake, Robert Blake, Roc Caivano, James M. Clark, Jr., Don Coates, Jan Coates, Elise Felton, Heather Frazer, Carol Fremont-Smith, Polly Guth, Penny Harris, Martha Jackson, Ann Judd, Phid Lawless, Julia Leisenring, Casey Mallinckrodt, Maude March, Sam McGee, Vittoria McIlhenny, Janneke Neilson, C.W. Eliot Paine, Polly Pierce, Nancy Putnam, Ken Savage, Beth Straus, Kathryn Suminsby, and Rodman Ward.

The creation of these books is a collaborative effort of many and under the aesthetic and creative eye of book designer and artist, Joanna Young and editor, Donna Gold.